HAMMER THROWING
by Alan Bertram

D1066841

The author dedicates this book to
Ernst Klement
of Trier in the Federal Republic of Germany
with grateful thanks for the encouragement
given over the years and the technical
knowledge so selflessly imparted during
his many visits to Trier.

First Edition	(J. Le Masurier)	1954
Second Edition	"	1959
Third Edition	"	1962
Fourth Edition	"	1963
Fifth Edition	"	1966
Sixth Edition	(H. Payne)	1969
Seventh Edition	(C. Johnson)	1984
This Edition	(A. Bertram)	1996

© British Athletic Federation
225A Bristol Road, Birmingham B5 7UB

ISBN 0 85134 131 4   1.5K/21K/01.96

Designed and printed by Reedprint Ltd,
Windsor, Berkshire, England.

About the Author

Northumbrian by birth, Alan Bertram moved to the capital where he joined the Metropolitan Police in 1960. Just over 30 years later he retired holding the rank of Chief Inspector and was awarded the M.B.E. He had competed regularly for the Metropolitan Police, and had won his home county's championship with his favourite implement – the hammer.

Alan has now studied and coached hammer throwing for some 25 years, his chief mentor being Professor Ernst Klement of Trier in Germany, coach to three 80 metre throwers including the former world record holder, Karl-Hans Riehm. In 1977 Alan formed the West London Hammer School, the first club of its kind in the U.K. Its members include countless AAA and English Schools Championship medallists and record holders, including all three ESAA champions in both 1985 and 1986.

Alan has coached seven athletes who have won selection as G.B. Senior Internationals; in 1994 they achieved the first ever coach's double in winning the Senior National Championships for hammer for both men (Peter Vivian, 70.80m) and women (Lorraine Shaw, 59.58m). Alan was Event Coach for hammer for the G.B. Juniors 1987-90 and since then has been the Senior Event Coach. He has acted as Assistant Team Coach to G.B. teams on several occasions including the European Junior Championships of 1989 and the European Cup (Seniors) in 1994 and 1995.

CONTENTS

Acknowledgements

Cover photograph of Paul Head by Gray Mortimore/Allsport. Photographs of Peter Vivian by Mark Shearman (Official photographer to the British Athletic Federation). Photo sequence by Helmar Hommel. Photographs of Lorraine Shaw by Tony Hickey.

The author acknowledges with gratitude the help received from Lorraine Shaw and Peter Vivian in posing for photographs, and also the generous assistance given by Calvin Morriss (Biomechanics) of the Sports Science Faculty at Alsager Campus of Manchester Metropolitan University and by John Hillier (Strength Training).

Chapter 1

HISTORY

Early History

Hammer throwing has been traced by antiquarians to the Tailteann Games which took place at Tara in Ireland. The Games lasted from 1829 B.C. to 1168 A.D., outliving the early Olympic Games of 776 B.C. to 393 A.D. Little was written about the Tailteann Games until the "Book of Leinster" was compiled during the Twelfth Century. Here, it is recorded that Cuchulain, the Irish "Hercules", competed in the "Roth Cleas" or wheel event, "and spun at incredible speed until they parted company for the spoke to fly through the air and fall far beyond the marks of ordinary men". This is the first reference to a hammer-like competition.

The Encyclopaedia Britannica refers to the use of the sling and staff-sling as being the earliest military examples of adding force and range to the arm of the missile thrower. It credits the weight throwing tradition (one handed, two handed, overhead, from a run, from standing etc.) originally to Ireland. English records, it says, are scant, but the Scots are known to have used turning throws until as late as 1860 when they were discontinued because of danger to by-standers.

It is known that Edward II encouraged the sport and that Henry VIII was a proficient performer. Achmat, the last Turkish Emperor, was another ruler who placed the royal seal of approval on the event by competing in throwing the chariot wheel in Istanbul in 1662.

Hammer throwing became widely popular. Henry Peacham (the younger), in his book "The Complete Gentleman" published by Constable in 1622, felt obliged to warn the nobility against becoming too involved in a sport of the lower classes. He said, "Throwing the hammer and wrestling, I hold them exercises not so well beseeming nobility, but rather soldiers in a camp, and the prince's guard".

There is little doubt that the event lent itself to being a popular recreation among the working classes, particularly the farm labourer; indeed, the event related directly to their prowess at work.

The Cotswold Games were immensely popular between 1612 and 1852. In Robert Dover's improved version throwing the "sledge" was one of the events; a throw of 30.56m being recorded, but without a "run and follow".

Styles varied a great deal, but the most common was the pendulum style. The thrower stood side on to the landing area and swung the hammer in front of himself, like the pendulum of a clock, prior to release.

During the 1860's important changes in the event took place. The "sledge" was replaced by a spherical stone or iron head on a whippy wooden shaft (Scottish style). Donald Dinnie, a professional athlete of that era, is credited with being the first athlete to swing the hammer around his head. The event was included in the Oxford

University sports of 1860 and replaced Throwing the Cricket Ball in the "Varsity Match" in 1866.

During the last two decades of the nineteenth century, while the English experimented with a variety of rules which permitted first 7ft/2.135m and then 9ft/2.74m circles, 3ft 6ins/1.06m long wooden handles and metal handles, the Americans established their rules in 1887, i.e. 16lb/7.257kg hammer of 4ft/1.22m overall length, thrown from a 7ft/2.135m diameter circle – specifications which still apply today.

Modern Hammer Throwing

It is perhaps fitting that the cradle of modern day hammer throwing was dominated by Irish immigrants living in the United States of America, for it is the ancient Irish folklore hero Cuchulain who has the credit for starting it all off almost 4000 years ago.

Those early pioneers were a rather special breed with enormous physiques and were affectionately referred to as "whales". The best known were John Flannagan, Matt McGrath and Pat Ryan. Flannagan and McGrath were New York policemen. Between them they were responsible for raising the world record from 44.20m to 57.76m achieved by Ryan in 1913. Ryan's mark remained a record for a quarter of a century when it fell to Erwin Blask of Germany in 1938. Pat O'Callaghan, a home based Irishman, had thrown 59.54m in 1937, but this was never recognised as a world record since he belonged to the N.A.C.A., the Irish Association which was outlawed by the I.A.A.F.

These early day modern marks were accomplished off a dirt circle and the athletes wore shoes with spikes in the ball of the foot. The throw was executed by the athlete completing either one or two jump turns.

The technique was revolutionised in the 1930's by the German coach Sepp Christmann who devised the "heel/toe" method of turning, enabling the athlete to keep at least one foot in contact with the ground at all times. Two throwers working under his guidance, Karl Hein and Erwin Blask, were dominant for Germany at the 1936 Olympics, winning the gold and silver medals. Two years later, Blask broke the world record with a throw of 59.00m.

The first thrower to better 60 metres was Jozsef Csermak of Hungary; when winning the 1952 Olympic final in Helsinki he recorded 60.30m at the age of 20. Two months later, Sverre Strandli of Norway exceeded 200ft/61.24m in Oslo.

The 1952 Olympic Games were an important landmark in another respect. The Soviet Union, for the first time, was represented as a nation in the Olympic movement. Soviet athletes were, over the following years, to make a tremendous impact on the event and have continued to do so to date.

The first dominant Soviet hammer thrower was Michail Krivonosov, who won the European Championship of 1954 from Csermak and Strandli to formally establish the Russian tradition and lineage. For nine years Hal Connolly, an American of Irish descent, held back the Russian advance. Connolly had many epic duels with Krivonosov, and later Vasiliy Rudenkov. He won the 1956 Olympic Games, defeating

Krivonosov, and set six world records from 1956 to 1965. Connolly was the first athlete to beat the 70 metre barrier, recording 71.24m in 1965, his last world record.

Despite Connolly's records, it was Romuald Klim of the Soviet Union and Gyula Zsivotsky of Hungary who were the dominant forces in the 1960's. Klim won the 1964 Olympics and Zsivotsky went on to win the 1968 Olympic Games. Klim, who was coached by Krivonosov, was an excellent technician, and set a world record of 74.52m in 1969.

Klim's record lasted only three months, and he was succeeded by Anatoliy Bondarchuk as world record holder who recorded 75.50m. Bondarchuk was to have a tremendous influence on world hammer throwing in the years to come. He won the 1972 Olympics and was the pace setter for a group of highly talented athletes.

Despite the Soviet dominance at major championships during the 1970's, it was the Germans who held the world record for most of that decade. Without doubt, one of the most remarkable feats in the history of the event was that of Karl-Hans Riehm of Germany. Riehm broke the existing world record of Alexey Spiridonov, 76.66m, with all six of his throws at Rehlingen, Germany, on 19th May 1975. His series was an extraordinary 76.70m, 77.56m, 77.10m, 78.50m, 77.16m, 77.28m.

In July 1978, Boris Zaichuk of the Soviet Union became the first to break the 80 metres barrier, setting a world record of 80.14m. A month later, Riehm reclaimed the record with a throw of 80.32m.

The arrival of Yuriy Sedykh and Sergei Litvinov heralded a new era in hammer throwing. Both these athletes, not big by any stretch of the imagination, displayed athleticism and skills hitherto not seen. They were completely dominant throughout the 1980's and were the sole custodians of the world record. The record of 86.74m set by Sedykh at the European Championships of 1986 remains unscathed. Like Riehm in 1980, Sedykh and Litvinov did not compete in the 1984 Olympics for political reasons arising out of the Afghanistan War. During their period of dominance both men were ably supported by Igor Nikulin and Yuriy Tamm.

More recently, politics have again played their part in the sport, with the separation of the Soviet Union into its several independent states. However, the very broad base of hammer involvement established over the years in the Soviet Union can still be witnessed at major world games Andrey Abduvaliyev of Tajikistan, Vasiliy Sidorenko of Russia and Igor Astopkovich of Belarus and several other younger throwers lead the way towards the year 2000.

British Throwing

Great Britain's only Olympic medal winner was Malcolm Nokes who set a British Record at 52.76m when winning the bronze medal at the 1924 Olympic Games. At the European Championships of 1946 Duncan Clark also won a bronze medal. Much through the work of Dennis Cullum the event gained popularity in the 1950's. A man with great passion and enthusiasm for the event, he formed the Hammer Circle of Great Britain. This exclusive club remains very active to this day.

In 1957, Michael Ellis, aged 19, became the first Briton to exceed 200ft (60.96m). During the following two years he rarely fell below that standard and was high in the world rankings of that period. Sadly, he never performed at his best in major championships. He finished 15th at the 1960 Olympic Games when a place in the first six would have been more appropriate. Regrettably, he retired before reaching his full potential.

Ellis was succeeded by Howard Payne who was born in Rhodesia. Payne was a quite remarkable athlete, who reigned supreme in British hammer throwing for a decade or more, during which time he raised the British record to 69.24m in 1970; he was placed 10th at the 1968 Olympic Games and 8th at the European Championships of the following year.

Barry Williams was the first British athlete to break the 70 metre barrier (70.14m in 1973). Between 1972 and 1976 the British record was broken 13 times, Barry Williams, Ian Chipchase, Paul Dickenson and Chris Black all having custody of it at one time or another. Black was to finish in 7th place in the 1976 Olympic Games.

A similar situation prevailed in the 1980's when Bob Weir, Chris Black, Martin Girvan and Matt Mileham all laid claim to the record. The British record currently stands at 77.54m set by Girvan in 1984. Whilst never holding the record, David Smith, with a best of 77.30m, can probably claim to have the best competitive record of that decade. Smith won at the Commonwealth Games in 1986 and was runner up in 1990.

Paul Head, briefly challenged by Jason Byrne in 1992 with 73.80m, has been the outstanding thrower in the 1990's. Head has a best of 74.02m.

Women's Hammer

1994 was the year that women's hammer became recognised for world record purposes. Olga Kuzenkova of Russia has the honour of being the first world record holder with a mark of 66.84m.

Over the past few years the event has gained in popularity in several countries, Britain included. It is no surprise to find that many of the world's leading women throwers come from those countries that formed the former Soviet Union and Eastern Europe. There is little doubt that they will feature well to the fore when the event is included in major championships.

There is considerable interest in Britain in the women's event, both at Senior and Junior level. At the time of writing Lorraine Shaw holds the British record with 64.90m and Britain too should be well represented in future championships.

Chapter 2

PHYSICAL ATTRIBUTES

Perhaps the most important prerequisite for throwing the hammer is the ability to rotate at speed; this, coupled with weight and strength, are important attributes of the successful hammer thrower. Although not essential, hammer throwers do tend to be reasonably tall (6ft/1.83m).

Mitchell, Flannagan, McGrath & Ryan (the original "whales") were very large men judged by the standards of the time. Ryan was the tallest at 6ft 2ins/1.88m and weighed 250lbs/113.6kg. Even McGrath, the shortest at 5ft 11ins/1.81m, weighed 248lbs/112.7kg. Despite their size they were all reputed to be very athletic. Flannagan long jumped 6.70m and triple jumped 14.04m.

The world class hammer thrower of today is of similar stature. The average height and weight of the finalists at the 1992 Barcelona Olympic Games was 6ft. 2^{1}/$_{2}$ins/1.89m and 246lb/112kg. The average age was 30 years – extremely mature athletes. Modern day hammer throwers at world class levels do vary. Sergei Litvinov, with a best of 86.04m, is 5ft. 10^{1}/$_{2}$ins/1.80m and 220lbs/100kg, whereas Yuriy Tamm, with a best of 84.40m is 6ft 4^{1}/$_{2}$ins/1.93m. and 264lbs/120kg. The general trend however has been towards taller and heavier throwers.

British throwing at the top has displayed similar trends. Of the smaller athletes, Peter Vivian is a fraction under 6ft/1.83m and 224lbs/102kg., whilst Paul Head is 6ft 4^{1}/$_{2}$ins/1.93m and 253lbs/115kg.

Whether or not the athlete possesses the desirable qualities within his physical make-up, he must work hard to develop the greatest leg and back strength that he possibly can. He must also develop great "hammer strength" which will permit him to maintain a sound throwing position, and to remain relaxed under immense physical pressure.

Chapter 3

A GUIDE TO THE RULES

Experience shows that it is very wrong to assume that all field event athletes and coaches fully understand the rules of their event. It is not the remit of this booklet to explain them in detail. A copy of the BAF "Rules for Competition" can be purchased from the British Athletics Bookcentre, 5 Church Road, Bookham, Surrey, KT23 3PN. However, the basic rules can be summarised as follows:

1. The throw is made from a 7ft/2.135m diameter circle into a 40° landing area.

2. In making the attempt the thrower must commence from a stationary position inside the circle, and remain within its confines until the implement has landed.

3. The athlete must then leave the circle from the rear half.

4. The competition placing will be assessed according to the thrower's best throw. If he/she ties with another competitor, the tie will be resolved by referring to the next best throw.

5. Touching the ground with the implement at any stage of the throw does not invalidate the throw.

Restarting a Throw

The most troublesome of these rules relates to the thrower's right to interrupt the throw and restart it. This opportunity is permitted in all throwing events. The rule therefore has the following qualifications special to the hammer throw.

1. It shall not be considered a foul throw if the head of the hammer touches the ground, or the top of the iron band, when the competitor makes the preliminary swings or turns; but if, having so touched the ground, or the top of the iron band, the competitor stops throwing so as to begin a trial again, this shall count as a failure.

2. Provided that in the course of the trial the foregoing Rules have not been infringed, a competitor may interrupt a trial once started, may lay down the hammer and may leave the circle before returning to a stationary position and beginning a fresh trial.

On Landing

For a valid throw the hammer *head* must fall *completely* within the inner edges of lines marking a sector of 40° set out on the ground.

All measurement must be made from the nearest edge of the mark first made in the ground by the head of the hammer, to the inner edge of the circle, along a line drawn from the centre of the circle.

Protection

The hammer thrower is permitted to wear a protective glove. The glove must be smooth on back and front, and the tips of the fingers, other than the thumb, must be exposed.

Treating the Circle

A competitor must not spray or spread any substance on the surface of a throwing circle nor on his shoes.

Chapter 4

EQUIPMENT AND ITS CARE

Hammers

Hammer heads are made of solid iron, brass or any metal not softer than brass, or a shell of such metal filled with lead or other solid material. They must be spherical in shape.

Hammer handles vary in shape, size and weight and are chosen by throwers according to the 'feel' or suitability to a particular hammer.

Hammer wires should be made from No. 11 Steel Wire Gauge spring-steel wire. This is to prevent distortion during use. Most manufacturers make several models of hammer, each having different types and sizes of heads and handles, and therefore requiring different lengths of wire in order to attain the maximum permitted overall length of 121.5 cm. measured to the inner edge of the handle.

The spring-steel wire is quite brittle and can be damaged on landing, especially in very dry conditions. When a kink appears in the wire, this is a sign that it has weakened and is liable to break. It is therefore safest to replace it immediately. For the same reason hammers should be stored hanging from a hook so that the weight of the head keeps the wire pulled straight.

The spindle which attaches the wire to the hammer head will also require care and attention. It should be kept free of mud, in order to prevent jamming. The spindle should be oiled to keep it in good working order.

The hammer shall conform to the specifications shown in the table opposite.

Gloves

As indicated in the section on rules, a glove is necessary to protect the hand. Right handed throwers need to wear a glove on their left hand, and left handed throwers on their right hand. They can be ordered from good sports shops, but the best means is by ordering direct; particulars are available within the advertising columns of "Athletics Weekly".

For the beginner, he/she may improvise by using either an ordinary leather glove or a heavy duty rubber glove. These are only really suitable during the early stages of learning when the hammer is not being thrown very far.

Finger Tape

Even when gloves are worn a fair amount of skin damage is sustained by the hand in contact with the hammer handle. Blisters and calluses will form. To keep the damage to a minimum, the athlete can tape each finger individually with adhesive tape, or P.V.C. insulation tape. The latter is best because of its smooth shiny nature which reduces chafing inside the glove – which is the main cause of the problem.

Men	Seniors		Juniors	
	Minimum	Maximum	Minimum	Maximum
Weight complete	7.26kg		6.25kg	
Length of hammer	117.5cm	121.5cm	117.5cm	121.5cm
Diameter of head	110mm	130mm	99mm	126mm
	Under 17		Under 15	
	Minimum	Maximum	Minimum	Maximum
Weight complete	5kg		4kg	
Length of hammer	117.5cm	121.5cm	116cm	119.5cm
Diameter of head	95mm	118mm	95mm	110mm
Women	Seniors		Juniors	
	Minimum	Maximum	Minimum	Maximum
Weight complete	4kg		4kg	
Length of hammer	116cm	119.5cm	116cm	119.5cm
Diameter of head	95mm	110mm	95mm	110mm
	Under 17			
	Minimum	Maximum		
Weight complete	4kg			
Length of hammer	116cm	119.5cm		
Diameter of head	95mm	110mm		
Veterans	Men 40-49		Men 50-59	
	Minimum	Maximum	Minimum	Maximum
Weight complete	7.26kg		6kg	
Length of hammer	117.5cm	121.5cm		
Diameter of head	110mm	130mm		
	Men 60-69		Men 70 & over	
	Minimum	Maximum	Minimum	Maximum
Weight complete	5kg		4kg	
Length of hammer	117.5cm	121.5cm	116cm	119.5cm
Diameter of head	95mm	118mm	95mm	110mm

Footwear

For good throwing a correct type of shoe is essential. Special shoes (see Plate 1) having leather uppers and a wrap-over rubber sole are necessary if the athlete intends to take the event seriously. Because of their specialist nature, these shoes are expensive and not always easy to obtain. Some brands are more hard wearing than others. The shoes can be re-soled and it is worthwhile finding a cobbler sufficiently skilled to do the job. For the beginner a gym shoe is ideal.

Plate 1

Chapter 5

GENERAL PRINCIPLES OF HAMMER THROWING TECHNIQUE

The technical basis of the throw is best considered under the following component parts:

1. Grip
2. Starting Position.
3. Swings.
4. Entry or transition phase.
5. Turns.
6. Delivery.

Whilst it is necessary to be aware of the above mentioned component parts of the throw, it is important that the coach and athlete evaluate the throw as a whole as opposed to breaking it into its various parts.

In the text which follows, all references pertain to the right handed thrower and references which require to be changed for left handed thrower are underlined.

At the rear of the booklet is a photo-sequence of the World Record Holder, Yuri Sedykh. (86.74m). This record was set in 1986, but Sedykh remains to date the model of technical correctness and consistency. Throughout the following chapters reference will be made from time to time to a particular part of the throw within this photo-sequence.

General Aspects

Hammer is very much a rhythm event, in which it is necessary for the thrower to blend his movements with those of the missile in order to achieve peak performance. The champion thrower needs to have an inborn feel for the hammer and will have to work hard to develop this further throughout training.

This will have been achieved when he is able to use his legs and lower torso ahead of his arms and shoulders to balance the increasing outward pull of the hammer, enabling him to absorb it through his legs, buttocks and lower back. This ability, is fundamental to the event and therefore must be recognised by both coach and athlete.

1. Grip

For a right handed thrower, the athlete holds the hammer handle in the gloved left hand so that the grip rests along the middle pads of the fingers; thereafter it is covered by the right hand. (Plates No. 2a/2b on page 24.)

2. Starting Position

There are several variations; however, the current World Record Holder, Yuri Sedykh, keeps it simple. The thrower stands at the rear of the circle, with his back facing towards the throwing area. The feet are placed approximately shoulder width apart. The hammer head is placed towards the rear of the circle and to the right of the thrower. The athlete then adopts the grip (Plate No. 4 page 24).

3. **Swings**

Basically the purpose of the swings is five fold, i.e.:

i) To put the hammer in motion.

ii) To establish the rhythm of the throw.

iii) To establish the plane of the hammer.

iv) To establish the correct position of the low point immediately prior to entry.

v) To establish good balance.

The number of swings varies, depending on the athlete. Generally speaking, however, most experienced throwers consider two to be the optimum number. Novice throwers might find it helpful to try three swings.

The plane of the hammer is highly important. A thrower using three turns must swing with a slightly steeper plane than the athlete who uses four turns.

To establish the correct plane, the hammer head ought not to rise too much above the thrower's head during the preliminary swings and should be just below knee height at the low point. This will ensure a relatively flat plane at the start of the throw.

As a general rule, the correct plane is that which permits the thrower to enter the turns without hindrance and then link smoothly with the plane of the first turn. This is most effectively accomplished when the plane at the final swing is such that its low point occurs around an azimuth angle of 330° (1 o'clock). (See Diagram 1).

Because of its rotational, gyroscopic nature, a very fine awareness of balance is required of the thrower. This balance, or lack of it as the case may be, is most apparent during the turns, but is established from the very beginning of the swings.

Throughout the swings, the moving hammer has a tendency to pull the thrower with it, and this must be countered by moving the hips away from the hammer while absorbing the force by slightly flexing the knees. In this manner the thrower opposes the position of the hammer with his body and sets up a continuing counter clockwise rotation of his hips ahead of the hammer. Thus the thrower's weight begins to move left while the hammer head is still at its high point, just prior to the start of the entry phase. In this way a balance point slightly left of centre is established for the turns that follow.

Now a little more about the execution of the swings. The main generator of power during the swings is the hips; it is a hip movement and not an arm movement. The initial movement of the hammer head to the front is accompanied by a shifting of the body weight from the right leg to the left. The shoulders will unwind to face the front, as will the arms.

Most throwers look off to the right during the swings at an azimuth angle of 330° (1 o'clock).

Reference points using
(a) the 'clock' system   (b) compass points

REAR OF THE CIRCLE

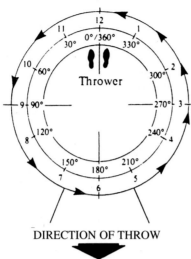

DIRECTION OF THROW

Diagram 1

When the hammer head reaches the front, the thrower bends his <u>left</u> arm as the hammer head passes the body. The hands must then be brought up close to the top of the head (they should not go beyond the centre of the head) as the hammer passes behind on the <u>left</u> hand side of the thrower. Body weight must now be shifted back to the <u>right</u>.

Hips and shoulders must now be turned towards the throwing area on the <u>right</u> hand side, the shoulders stretching back approximately to an azimuth angle of 180° (6 o'clock).

This movement is to be completed twice (or three times) prior to the commencement of the entry.

As the hammer is stretched back to its furthest extremity on the final swing, just prior to sweeping into the entry, it ought to be like a coiled spring. Igor Nikulin, the Russian thrower, compares it to a bow and arrow, just prior to the release of the arrow.

As mentioned earlier, the low point of the hammer head is to the right of the thrower during the swings. Upon entry to the first turn, the low point is opposite the <u>right</u> foot, azimuth angle 330° (1 o'clock). {Sed. 7}

The Entry – Transition Phase

The athlete must think of the entry actually starting at the high point of the final swing. The thrower begins to lower his centre of gravity and actively unwinds his body from the coiled spring situation. {Sed. 1-7}

When the low point of the hammer is reached – azimuth angle approximately 330° (1 o'clock), the hammer head must then be worked through to the entry or start position. This occurs when the shoulder axis is parallel to the hip and leg axis. In other words, when the hammer is directly in front of the thrower – azimuth angle of 0/360° (12 o'clock). {Sed. 8-9}.

Both arms will be stretched outwards and will form an isosceles triangle {Sed. 9} which must be maintained throughout the entire throw.

At the critical time of entry, the right hip and leg should be braced {Sed 8/9} and both legs should be in a bandy (or bowed) position with both heels inside. Ernst Klement, the world renowned coach from Germany, refers to this as the Charlie Chaplin position and it explains the situation very well indeed.

The transitional period from the swings to the entry is one of the most difficult elements of the throw and, if not executed properly, will have an effect on the entire throw.

The Turns

For conventional throwers, (three turns), the athlete turns on the centre part of the left heel applying considerable pressure. The thrower also applies pressure through the ball of the right foot as he moves into the first turn {Sed 8-11}. For throwers using four turns, the movement is carried out on the ball of the left toe as opposed to the heel. It should be noted, however, that there are some world class throwers who can do four conventional turns within the confines of the throwing circle.

The hip and shoulder axis remain parallel at this stage and the thrower looks in the direction of the hammer, a situation that must be continued throughout the throw. In the first turn the upper body is slightly inclined toward the front during this movement. {Sed. 8-11}.

At this stage the thrower is in the double support phase (both feet in contact with the ground). The breaking of contact of the right foot with the ground differs between athletes, but there is a critical time when this must take place and this occurs around azimuth angle of 80° to 90° (9 o'clock) {Sed 12}. As a general rule, the right foot must break contact prior to 90° in the first turn. Slower throwers must break contact with the right foot earlier than the swifter throwers.

The thrower continues to pivot on the left heel (or in the case of a four turner, on the left toe of the support leg) and is now in the single support phase (one foot in contact with the ground).

Turning on the left heel will continue until an azimuth angle of approximately 180° (6 o'clock) (not more), whereupon the pressure is transferred from the left heel to the ball of the outer edge of the support foot. The turn is completed by the right leg stepping quickly over the left ankle, ensuring the thighs are kept close, and the right foot again making contact with the ground {Sed. 13-15}.

The Double Support Phase

The 'double support phase' commences at the time the right foot makes contact with the ground and ends when it is lifted from the ground. It is the main phase of acceleration of the hammer. The athlete must, throughout the turns, strive for positions which permits this to happen, thus allowing the hammer speed to increase right up to its release. An early landing of the ball of the right foot must take place at the end of each turn, azimuth angle 270° approximately (3 o'clock). The eyes of the thrower must be looking in the direction of the hammer. The landing must be powerful and active.

At the time of landing the thrower is in the lowest position due to the flexion of the left leg at the end of the single support position {Sed 19- end of 2nd turn}. Upon landing at the end of each turn, acceleration is brought about by applying pressure through the arms, shoulder girdle and trunk as well as the legs. This continues until the shoulders and hips are again aligned at the front. The ball of the right foot must be active during this operation. A quick plant of the left heel, positioned inside under the body is essential for the efficiency of the next turn.

The entire body must work as a single unit as it turns to the left. The thrower must achieve as large a radius as is possible on the left hand side. The movement must not be rushed.

Each subsequent turn is executed almost identically to the first. For four turn throwers who start with a toe turn, the 2nd, 3rd and 4th turns will be carried out on the heel of the left foot identically to that of the conventional three turn throwers. Due to increasing speed of the hammer throughout the turns, the right foot, generally speaking, breaks contact with the ground earlier. This again differs between athletes, but the more speedy gifted thrower is able to keep contact with the ground a little longer.

The Single Support Phase

The single support phase commences when the right foot breaks contact with the ground and terminates when it again makes contact with the ground. During this phase, the hammer thrower turns through the force of inertia created during the double support phase. To ensure that reduction of speed of the hammer head is kept to a minimum, the thrower must seek for relaxation of the shoulders and arms. The hammer must be allowed to run freely and unimpeded.

As previously stated, the thrower continues to turn on the heel of the left foot until an azimuth angle of just under 180° (6 o'clock), whereupon the pressure is transferred from the heel to the ball of the left foot. Upon the hammer reaching its high point, the thrower lowers the centre of gravity thereby counteracting the upward and outward pull of the hammer. This is achieved by bending or collapsing the left knee underneath the hammer {Sed. 14,18,22}. With the experienced and talented thrower, the hammer head speed will increase at the latter part of the single support phase as a result of this, just prior to the placement of the right foot, which commences the start of the double support position.

The Delivery

The delivery is a continuation of the turns and serves to give the final acceleration to the hammer. The delivery phase begins with the active touch down of the right foot at the end of the final turn. As in the previous turns, the athlete's centre of gravity is at its lowest. In order that the hammer accelerates to its maximum until the final low point is reached, the planting of the right foot must be an extremely active movement. The right foot continues to work in the throwing direction, during which time the body torque previously established is released. The full extension of the legs must not come into effect until just prior to the low point of the hammer head being reached. If this is not adhered to, an important part of the acceleration path will be lost.

Upon the low point of the hammer head being passed, the right leg continues to push the right hip towards the left, against a braced left hand side of the body. The left leg is then fully extended with the left foot kept 'flat' on the ground, thus ensuring a strong platform for delivery or release of the hammer. {Sed. 24 -27}. The movement is completed when the pelvis axis is in line with the throwing direction when the pelvis is stopped suddenly. This causes the transmission of forces of the lower body chain to the trunk and arms. The movement is completed with the hands high above the head. {Sed. 25-27}.

Chapter 6

BIOMECHANICAL PRINCIPLES OF HAMMER THROWING

Many coaches agree that the technique of the thrower would seem to be the discriminating factor between athletes at the highest level. Therefore, an understanding of the way in which an athlete's movements affect the motion of the hammer is crucial to the athlete's success. Sports biomechanics is the scientific discipline that is concerned with the way in which an athlete generates force and the effects of these forces (the movement of the athlete). Owing to the complexity of the hammer throw, biomechanical analysis systems have been used to give the coach and athlete a view of the throw in greater detail than can be seen with the naked eye. In addition, an increased amount of information regarding specific aspects of the throw that are considered to be important can also be provided.

The following sections are intended to introduce the reader to the factors that may limit the performance of an athlete and provide an explanation of why even a limited understanding of the biomechanics of the event could be useful to the coach.

Distance Thrown

After the athlete releases the hammer, the only forces that act on it are the pull of gravity and air resistance. Unlike throwing events where the implement is relatively aerodynamic, such as javelin or discus, the hammer is unaerodynamic and creates little or no lift forces which work to lengthen the flight time. This puts greater emphasis for success on the release conditions which affect the distance thrown that are directly under the athlete's control. In order of importance these conditions are the release speed, angle and height.

Release Speed

Assuming that the hammer is released at an angle of approximately 45°, the relationship between the release speed of the hammer and the distance it will travel is basically as follows:

$$\text{DISTANCE THROWN} = \frac{\text{RELEASE SPEED}^2}{10}$$

Because of the squared term in the release speed, this tells us that a relatively small increase in release speed can result in a quite dramatic increase in distance thrown. For example, for a throw where the release speed is approximately 27m/s (a throw of about 70 metres), an increase in release speed of 1m/s can result in an increase in the throw distance of as much as 5m. In the light of this, the generation of the maximum possible release speed becomes by far the most important goal of the athlete.

Release Angle

Because the hammer is released from a point above that at which it lands, the ideal release angle is below 45°, at approximately 43°-44°. Deviations from this angle do not have a vast effect on the distance thrown. It has been reported that a move of 5° from the optimum angle would reduce the range of the throw by approximately 1m. Probably of greater importance is the effect that moving the hammer through a different path in an effort to alter the release angle would have on the release speed. To illustrate this point in a different way, elite shot putters tend to project the shot at release angles less than the optimum (which is about 43°), probably because their ability to generate force and increase the release speed of the shot is improved in this way.

Release Height

Nearly all athletes release the hammer at shoulder height; the release height is therefore governed by the height of the athlete as much as any technical factor. Changes in the release height have only marginal effects on the distance thrown; Calculations suggest that increases in the release height result in similar increases in throw distance. This means that increasing the release height from 1.7m to 1.9m (all else remaining equal) would improve the distance thrown by about 20cm.

Factors Affecting the Generation of Release Speed

From a theoretical standpoint, the factors that affect the speed of the hammer can be summarised by the following equation:

$$v = r\omega$$

Where $\quad v$ = linear speed; r = radius; ω = angular velocity.

The linear speed of the hammer is otherwise known as the tangential speed, and would be the straight-line speed at which the hammer would leave the thrower's grasp should he let it go at any instant. (The release speed is hence a linear speed). The angular velocity of the hammer gives an idea of the turning speed of the thrower, and the radius of rotation is the distance of the hammer head from the point in space about which both the thrower and the hammer are rotating. Interpretation of the equation leads us to this conclusion: that to attain the maximum possible release speed, the radius of rotation and the angular velocity of the hammer should be as high as possible. In theory this is correct. As we shall see in the following section, the thrower should adopt the body positions that result in the best combination of radius and turning velocity, even if one component is compromised for the benefit of the other. This is simply because of the practicalities of hammer throwing since the body position in which the thrower is strongest, and best able to work the hammer, might not always maximise both the radius and the angular velocity.

Maintenance of a Long Radius

As the length of the hammer wire is fixed, so the radius of rotation of the hammer is dependent upon the body position of the athlete. In particular, it is the position of the thrower's shoulder and hip joints that have the greatest influence on the radius. For instance, if the thrower leans forward at the waist and inclines the trunk, and also reaches forward with the hands, the radius will be increased. Owing to the increasing tilt of the hammer plane through the throw, the positions of the thrower's knees as he lowers and raises the body also affect the length of the radius. Because the body position of the thrower changes during the different phases of each turn, the radius will also change accordingly. Naturally, this will in turn affect the linear speed of the hammer. This issue is addressed in the following sections. For ease of understanding, all body positions are described as if the athlete is a right handed thrower.

Single Support Phase

During the single support phase, the thrower has only his body weight and the frictional force that can be generated by the support leg to affect the motion of the hammer. It follows that the angular velocity of the hammer will be reduced in this phase, thus resulting in a loss of overall linear speed. However, when in single support the thrower's body position may be described as being flexed at the shoulders and flexed at the knees. This has the benefit of lengthening the radius, which offsets some of the negative effects of the reduced angular velocity, resulting in only a small loss of linear speed. These positions should be emphasised at an early stage in the athlete's development, particularly with regard to strengthening of the lower back and legs to generate the muscular force necessary for the athlete to adopt these body positions.

Of much importance during the single support phases is the movement of the athlete's lower body. By moving the right knee in close to that of the left immediately after right foot take off, the athlete is able to rotate the lower body ahead of the shoulders and so prepare the upper body for accelerating the hammer during the double support phase.

To summarise, the thrower should be concerned with staying on the hammer with the body during single support phase (arms straight and the hammer wire at right angles to the line of shoulders), and accelerating the lower body ahead of the upper body prior to the right foot touch down. This will create tension in the musculature of the midriff in preparation for double support, and also serve to minimise the loss of hammer speed during the single support by keeping the radius as long as possible.

Double Support Phase

If the thrower can utilise the single support phase to arrive at right foot touch down in a position where the hips are rotated ahead of the shoulders, then the athlete is in a position to generate a torque to accelerate the upper body and, therefore, the hammer. This is an important mechanism as, by unwinding the mid-section of the body, the thrower has a method of increasing the angular velocity of the hammer without the detrimental effects of dragging.

The straightening of the left leg during double support to move the hips along a path opposite to that of the hammer is also an important movement during the double support phases, its benefits being two-fold. Firstly, by moving in opposition to the hammer, the thrower creates greater tension in the wire, so promoting greater acceleration. Secondly, the unwinding of the upper body to re-align with the hips is facilitated by this movement.

Owing to the lowering of the athlete's arms and the straightening of the legs, the radius will naturally be decreased during the double support because the hammer head is moved closer to the axis of rotation. However, if the thrower can time his forceful unwinding of the torso and straightening of the <u>left</u> leg appropriately, then the increase in the angular velocity will outweigh any detrimental effects of reducing the radius. The overall result will be an increase in the hammer's linear speed.

The Delivery

World class athletes have been shown to accelerate the hammer greatly during the delivery, making this an extremely important phase of the throw. Yuri Sedykh, for example, was reported to increase the speed of the hammer by 6.6m/s during the delivery of his world record throw.

The coach's instructions to an athlete regarding his movements during this phase should be carefully worded as the action of standing up is not as simple as it seems. At all times during the throw, the athlete should be attempting to move his body (specifically the hips) in opposition to the motion of the hammer because this acts to increase the force in the cable. Applying these thoughts to the delivery means that the thrower should indeed forcefully extend the legs, but in such a way that the hammer's motion is always opposed. For example, the legs should begin to extend upon the <u>right</u> foot touch down (as in the turns) when the hammer is moving downwards. Then, as the hammer passes through the low point and begins its upward path, the emphasis passes to the trunk and shoulders, where the former is hyper extended and the latter flexed. Collectively, these movements will rapidly increase the force in the cable, promoting acceleration of the hammer, resulting in the order of release speed necessary to attain long distance throws.

Chapter 7

TECHNICAL TRAINING

So far this booklet has concentrated almost entirely upon the technical and theoretical aspects of the event. In this chapter we shall begin to turn our attention to its more practical considerations, beginning with the earliest development of hammer skills and awareness.

It is important that the development of the technique 'criteria' mentioned in the chapter on "General Principles of Hammer Throwing" should take place as soon as possible in the training of a hammer thrower.

Teaching the Beginner

The manner in which a thrower is introduced to the event is extremely important. A good base must be established from the outset in order that the more advanced techniques can be tackled successfully.

Coaches who have the opportunity of selecting throwers should look for fairly tall athletes who are fast. Fast means capable of rotating quickly around the foot or heel of the left leg, through push off, swing and plant of the foot of the right leg. *There is no direct relationship between the ability to move fast in a straight line and in a rotating direction.*

In hammer throwing, the most promising athletes are those who are able to rotate at speed with hammers of varying weights.

If the athlete is young and on the short side, then the coach might deem it appropriate to introduce the athlete to the event with a shorter implement. A metre overall length or even 80cm is ideal. It is not advocated that less that 80cm be used. Stick throwing, shot throwing and other drills play an extremely important role in a beginner's learning and development.

In addition to teaching the basics of hammer throwing (preliminary swings, turns and delivery) the coach must ensure that:

i)   A general physical preparation base is created.

ii) Co-ordination is improved.

iii) That the athlete becomes used to regular training and thereby becoming disciplined.

It is useful for the beginner to have an understanding of the basic elements of the technique. This can best be done by explaining the technique by way of photo-sequence, drawings and videos.

Each individual coach has his/her own method and variations on the basic theme, a summary of which is as follows:

1. **Teaching the Swings and Delivery**

    1.1 Teach the correct grip (Plate Nos. 2a/2b on page 24)

21

1.2 Explain the start position.

1.3 Get the athlete to swing the hammer, having first demonstrated how this is done. The best method is by using a light hammer (one which the pupil can handle with ease). Take the hammer solely in the right hand and swing forwards, upwards and back, and repeat. (Plate No. 3)

1.4 Having successfully mastered swinging the hammer with one arm, the thrower can then adopt the proper grip and stance and swing in the orthodox manner with two arms. (Plate No. 4)

1.5 Once the athlete can swing he/she can then deliver over his/her left shoulder on the high side.

2. Teaching the Turns

It is extremely easy to teach the turns without a hammer. This is best done by demonstration and verbal instructions. The main points to emphasise are:

2.1 Proper stance. The balance points, which are the heel of the turning left foot and the toe of the right foot.

2.2 The need to turn on both feet simultaneously at the start (entry) and first half of the turn.

2.3 The raising of the left toe slightly as the foot pivots on the heel.

2.4 To turn a full 180° before transferring the weight from the heel to the toe of the left foot (single support balance position).

2.5 The action of the right leg in the second part of the turn should be active, both vertically and rotationally. The right knee should pass over and across the left leg with thighs close together. Active work must be confined to the right leg and right hip.

Having mastered the basics of the aforementioned 'dry turns', progress can quickly be made with a pick-axe handle, a metal rod, or a weights disc. (The weights disc is held in front with half bent arms).

For the purpose of this booklet, we shall use a pick-axe handle.

2.6 Start in a central position.
Seated, knees bowed, heels turned inwards (Plate No. 5).

2.7 Turn 180° to the balance position on the heel of the left foot and ball of the right foot (Plate No.6).
N.B. When the thrower is actually throwing the hammer, he would have ceased right foot contact with the ground at azimuth angle 90° or less (9 o'clock).

2.8 Action now as in 2.5. The landing of the right foot and start of the double support phase is at approximately azimuth angle 270° (3 o'clock). (Plate No.7).

2.9 The athlete then pivots on the ball of both feet back to the initial start position (Plate No. 5).

These drills must be repeated many times.

N.B. Initially, the coach might find it desirable for the novice thrower to complete the turn from 2.7 to 2.9 in one movement, thus avoiding stopping at 2.8. However, it is of paramount importance that the correct positions are experienced and repeated at an early stage of the thrower's career.

Now to throwing the hammer with turns. For the beginner it is a difficult task to join up the swings and entry with the turns when the athlete is concentrating on the difficult footwork. It is at this stage that the athlete and coach must be extremely patient.

The conventional method is perhaps the best means of progressing the technique at this stage, i.e. adopting the correct stance and grip; thereafter, executing two or three swings, going into the turns and then delivering the hammer.

Other Methods

As the thrower grows in confidence and experience, other training methods can be used. A lighter than normal hammer should be used for ease of movement and better learning:

2.10 Swinging the hammer with the right arm as in 1.3. (Plate No. 3) and then turning whilst keeping the hammer only in the right hand. Once confidence is gained, the athlete can then place the left hand on the right (reverse grip) at the point where the swings change to entry, (Plate No. 8.), and then turn with the hammer extended on two arms. Alternatively, the athlete can grip the right wrist with the left hand prior to the time of entry (Plate No. 9) and turn in this manner.

This drill can also be done by swinging and turning with the hammer in the left hand.

2.11 By passing the hammer from hand to hand (right to left) around the waist (Plates 10/11/12). After a few rotations, when the hammer has gained momentum, the athlete takes a two handed grip on the hammer handle and commences to turn. This is also a valuable drill for experienced athletes.

2.12 Another method is by the coach throwing the hammer in its correct path from the right of the athlete. It is essential, however, that the coach places the hammer into the correct orbit. During the development of the athlete, each of the aforementioned drills can be used with great effect to master the complex skill of timing the entry, which is all important to ensure a good throw.

3. **Linking the Swings to the Turns**

Once the athlete can handle the basic rudiments of a "heel-toe" turn, it is then essential that he/she progresses as quickly as possible to three, four or more turns. This however, depends very much upon the skill level of the athlete.

To give the athlete confidence, it is best done by adding one extra turn at a time and completing the throw with a delivery. It is important for the development of the athlete

Plate 2a

Plate 2b

Plate 3

Plate 4

Plate 5

Plate 6

Plate 7

Plate 8

Plate 9

Plate 10

Plate 11

Plate 12

26

Plate 13

Plate 14

Plate 15

Plate 16

that he/she learns to do multiple turning at an early stage. This is best done on a concrete strip if one is available; however, safety must be adhered to at all times.

When the athlete is able to throw in a stable manner from three or four turns, and again this will be determined by the skill level of the athlete, he/she can be taught about the length of the double support phase in each turn. It must be emphasised early on in the thrower's career that it is essential that the right foot breaks contact with the ground, thereby going into the single support phase, prior to the hammer reaching an azimuth angle of 90° (9 o'clock). Attention must also be drawn to the fact that each successive turn must be faster than the previous one.

B. The 'Short Hammer' Method

The short hammer method is perhaps a better means of teaching the event at the outset in schools or where there are large groups of athletes. It must be said, however, that this is no substitute for the real implement. This method is also suitable where the throwing area is restricted.

A short hammer is simply made by inserting two interlocked 'D' shackles, or a removable screw and bolt. (Plate No.13).

1. **Method**

    1.1 Teach the correct grip. (Plate 2a/b).

    1.2 Teach a standing throw in which the hammer is delivered over the left shoulder from a starting position just outside the right knee (Plates 14 and 15 on page 27).

    Points to emphasise are:

    (a) Sit by bending knees prior to starting.

    (b) To execute the delivery, pivot on the balls of both feet.

    (c) Attempt to deliver off a platformed left foot (entire foot on the ground) (Plate No. 15).

    (d) Use a rigorous leg lift.

    (e) Pelvis and shoulder axis in line with the throwing area at time of release (Plate No. 15).

    (f) Extend the arms overhead at the end of the movement.

    (g) Attempt to remain balanced throughout the entire movement.

    1.3 **Teach the Turns**

    (a) First by practising 'dry turns'; then moving on to turning with a pick-axe handle, metal rod or weights disc.

    (b) Progress onto the short hammer.

    (c) Proper turn and release.

2. Development

2.1 Introduce the turns.

2.2 Remove the 'D' shackle or nut/bolt and replace with a small length of nylon cord (breaking strain 500lbs/230kgs) tied in a knot which will not slip. Progressively make the nylon cord longer.

2.3 The swings can be taught when the hammer is long enough. Use the same method as in the teaching of the longer hammer.

The use of the short hammer is particularly suitable where practice areas are restricted. However, safety must be given top priority whatever the area.

Skill Improvement for Competent Throwers

The following routines are useful for developing the skills of the event. The drill for improving skills in the swings was created by Carl Johnson and I have found it most beneficial.

1. To Improve the Swings

Drill (i)

(a) Start with the hammer very close to the <u>right</u> foot (about 1ft/30cms outside the toes) with the hammer handle held vertically above the hammer head. (Plate No. 16).

(b) Slowly swing the hammer around the body in the correct manner, keeping it both near to the body and close to the ground.

(c) Feel what happens to the hips as the hammer passes to the high point side of the body.

(d) Having done that, feel what happens to the hips as the hammer passes to the low point side of the body.

(e) Once the countering action of the hips has been recognised, keep the swings going by a rotating hip action as opposed to an arm action.

Drill (ii)

(a) Swing the hammer normally. Attempt to feel the countering of the hips.

(b) When the hammer moves behind the body on the high point side, turn around to meet the hammer as early as possible when it appears again rear <u>right</u>.

(c) Move the <u>left</u> shoulder around to the <u>right</u> to facilitate this action.

(d) Pull the <u>right</u> elbow close to your side in order to keep the plane of the hammer as flat as possible.

(e) Don't make the mistake of forgetting to move the shoulders to the front as the hammer continues to circle. Failure to do this will cause the low point to remain too far to the right.

2. Improve the Turns

The following drills should be done initially without the hammer. They can be best practised with a pick-axe handle, metal rod, or a weights disc. The drills not only quickly develop the all important footwork, but enable the thrower to become aware of the body movement in relation to the hammer. The drills are particularly useful for the understanding of the final part of the single support phase and the start of the double support phase.

Assume the correct starting position with the knees slightly bent and bandy (bowed). Both heels should be turned inwards. Hold the pick-axe handle or other training aid in front. Ensure that the hip axis and shoulder axis are parallel (Plate No. 5). Apply pressure through the left heel and right toe. Turn to the 180° azimuth point (6 o'clock). Now transfer the weight to the left toe. **NOTE:** When actually throwing the hammer, the right foot must break contact with the ground prior to azimuth angle 90° (9 o'clock), but for the purpose of this drill it remains on the ground until the 180° balance point is reached (Plate No. 6).

During the second part of the turn, move the right leg actively around the left. Keep the thighs close together during the movement. Ensure that the right foot does not kick out. Even in the earlier stages of teaching the hammer, instruct the athlete to lower his/her centre of gravity just prior to the touch down of the right foot.

The athlete should land on the ball of the right foot with the toes of both feet pointing towards an azimuth angle of 270° (3 o'clock). At this point the centre of gravity of the athlete ought to be at its lowest. There should be a considerable flexion of the left leg, and the hips should be at their closest to the ground. Upon landing, the athlete must retain balance and stretch back from the training aid (Plate No. 7).

The athlete then continues the drill by pivoting on both feet, rising from the low position and ensuring that the left knee is being pushed away from the right. The drill continues until the athlete has returned to the front, azimuth angle 0°/360° (12 o'clock) and ought to be in the same position as that at the start of the drill, i.e. knees slightly bent and bowed, with both heels pointing inwards (Charlie Chaplin position). Again, the shoulder axis and hip axis are aligned (Plate No. 5).

The drill should be repeated many times over in many training sessions. It is essential that the coach be extremely attentive when these drills are being performed, making the necessary corrections and adjustments throughout.

Variations

As the athlete gains in confidence and becomes more skilled and competent, variations of the drill can be made. For example, commence the movement at azimuth angle 270° (3 o'clock) (Plate No. 7). Proceed to azimuth angle 180° (6 o'clock) (Plate No. 6). This must be one continuous movement. However, it must be stressed, that the athlete must ensure that all relevant positions are achieved. After a pause at azimuth angle 180° (6 o'clock), the athlete continues the movement to the start of the double support phase, azimuth angle 270° (3 o'clock) (Plate No. 7). Again, the drill should be repeated many times.

Delivery

Use of a pick-axe handle also affords an excellent means of learning and perfecting the delivery phase. Adopt a position as in Plate No. 7. Pivot on both feet for 180° and deliver. Delivery position as in Plate No. 15.

3. To Develop the Relationship between Swings and Successive Turns

The following combinations of swings in series are most beneficial to novice and experienced throwers alike. However, like all drills they must be carried out properly. They should be executed slowly and with great concentration throughout. The routine is particularly beneficial for perfecting the swings and entry into the turns. It is also extremely good for improving balance and footwork. A turning strip, whilst not essential, is desirable for these drills.

Drill 1   Swing followed by one turn, swing followed by one turn, etc. etc.

Drill 2   Swing followed by one turn, swing followed by two turns, repeating sequence.

Drill 3   Swing followed by two turns, swing – two turns, etc. etc.

Drill 4   Swing followed by one turn, swing – two turns, swing – three turns etc.

Several swings can be made between turning. It is important that the athlete is in control of the hammer.

When the drills become easy, the athlete can walk back along the strip, swinging the hammer, and repeat the sequence. Again, when the athlete becomes proficient, each drill can be completed with two or more turns and a full delivery. It is an excellent means of improving speed during the final turns, thus making way for an explosive delivery.

For the competent thrower who wishes to introduce a toe turn at the start of the throw, swing-turn drills afford an excellent learning skill. Naturally, the athlete will turn on the toe of the <u>left</u> foot on all first turns. This is a superb learning exercise for joining the first toe turn up with the second heel turn of the <u>left</u> foot.

NOTE: The thrower should strive to reproduce the positions achieved in the stick-drills when doing swing/turn drills.

Chapter 8

PLANNING TRAINING

Strength and size, whilst important, are insufficient in themselves to make a top class hammer thrower. The champion thrower must be possessed of considerable skill, explosive power and suppleness. Frequently, the five "S's" are spoken of in athletics, and in the following text I shall look at how these all important factors can be specifically developed for the hammer throw – train, don't strain, is the name of the game.

Skill

There is no substitute for skill. Specific skills must be performed when the athlete is fresh, and under no circumstances must the athlete be allowed to throw poorly due to fatigue or any other reason.

All major technique changes should be carried out during the winter months. As the competitive phase approaches, only small refinements should be considered. Having established the new skills, the coach must keep an ever watchful eye to ensure that they are maintained.

Whilst the whole skill must be of prime consideration, the throw must be broken into its component parts during the preparation and strength periods, and the whole – part – whole theory of learning adhered to.

Stamina

During the competition phase, the aerobic-endurance requirement is virtually nil. In training, however, the requirement is quite high and the athlete requires strength endurance for two vital areas.

(a) **Throwing.** Skill gains can only be made in a fatigue free situation. Therefore, it follows that the fitter the athlete, the more quality drills/throws may be made.

(b) **Strength/Conditioning Training.** There is no easy way to build strength. Long sessions are required in the weights room or gym. Naturally, the fitter the athlete, the more sets and repetitions he can perform, which lead to greater strength endurance.

The early part of the training year should be devoted to building up endurance (conditioning) and can consist of long runs of over 30 minutes, body weight exercises, circuit type and high repetition resistance training.

Speed

The development of speed can be achieved through sprinting, jumping, skipping, circuits and explosive use of resistance. For specific speed the athlete can use under-weight implements or heavy hammers on a short wire.

When throwing light hammers, those which are 0.5kg or 1.0kg lighter than the competitive implement are most appropriate. It should be noted that an implement which is too light can destroy the rhythm and timing of the throw. When throwing a heavy hammer for the purpose of speed, it is best done on a wire not exceeding 50cm.

In the period leading up to an important competition, the full weight implement should be used. If a variation is felt desirable, then a 6.75 kg. hammer would be ideal.

Suppleness

Hammer throwers should be power athletes, but if strength/size is achieved at the expense of mobility then the athlete may not throw further. High levels of mobility permit the most effective range of movement for optimum expression of skill.

General mobility exercises should be carried out daily if at all possible. A convenient way is for the athlete to perform mobility exercises in the warm-up for training.

In addition, units of training in which the aim is the improvement of flexibility should be planned and built into the athlete's schedule. They are best carried out in warm conditions indoors and partner work involving passive/active stretching is preferable.

A variety of suitable exercises can be found in the book 'Mobility Training' obtainable from the B.A.F. Bookcentre.

Strength

Strength is a critical component in power events. Undoubtedly, the best way to gain strength for throwing is by lifting heavy weights. But strength in itself will not overcome poor technique and lack of explosive power; all other components must be addressed.

Strength comes in many guises and may be gained in many different ways. Certainly what suits one individual may not suit another, and the coach/athlete must be prepared to adapt/change the programme where necessary. So many factors must be considered – home, family, job, environment, illness etc. all affect the performance.

Above all, the programme must be flexible. Whatever the method, the athlete must go down the road of progressive resistance training (PRT). To work with the same poundages, the same repetitions, the same sets and the same rest periods will quickly lead to boredom and staleness, and empirical evidence suggests that an actual regression takes place.

The athlete must be constantly and consistently challenged, both mentally and physically, and the programme must allow for this. Also empirical evidence suggests that to load/overload a muscle or group of muscles too much, too often, does not allow for repair after breakdown. Homeostasis must always be regained before the next loading. For example, after a very heavy/maximum loading session, perhaps the next two sessions on any particular muscle group could be with a considerable reduction in poundage, simply to flush the muscle through but still working it.

A system of change of Heavy-Light-Medium is recommended (see pages 35/36 for examples), and also changing the exercise somewhat from session to session to attack the muscles from different angles, e.g. Back Squat...........Front Squat.........Back Squat.

N.B. Always lift correctly and strictly respect the weights, and they will then respect you.

Definition

Heavy	=	100% plus
Medium	=	70% - 85%
Light	=	50% - 70%

This applies at all times, no matter whether you are doing a maximum for a set of 10 or a single lift, depending upon which week you are on in the programme.

These percentages need only apply to major exercises and not to assistance ones, although the reps. and poundage change will concern both during the cycles.

It is appropriate to work on micro-cycles of 14 days and even, if desirable, to do 4 weeks of 10's for example. Then this may be done as two weeks repeated twice.

A convenient way of planning may be as follows:

4 weeks of 10's
4 weeks of 5's
4 weeks of 3's   } Total 14 weeks
2 weeks of singling down to test improvement

Then repeated again, but the second cycle at a higher level than the first. This conveniently takes us from October to May.

If however, a later peak is required, i.e. July/August, it is possible to shorten the second two cycles to perhaps only two weeks of 10 reps. each and only one week of singles, involving then 11 weeks in each. This would allow for 3 cycles to be done from October to June.

Maintenance during the main competition phase must be done regularly, but be designed to fit around the competitions and hammer-specific training. A programme of some 5 sets of 5 repetitions at 60-75% is recommended.

A 3 cycle programme allows athletes to test themselves 3 times progressively which is possibly more ideal, certainly for a single periodised year. Constant testing must take place to identify areas of weakness or imbalances in strength so that they can be catered/adjusted for.

For the younger athlete, a word of caution must be voiced. The young athlete must *not* assume that lifting heavy weights from the start is a must. Such work can only be carried out after a long preparation. The road to heavy weights is by way of (a) body weight exercises, (b) circuit training of a general nature, (c) circuit training combined with all-round strength exercises – perhaps on multi-gym equipment, (d) learning a good technique with a moderately loaded barbell for the specialised weight lifting programme that lies ahead.

The preparation period for the young athlete can last several years, and the specialist hammer thrower may not start lifting heavy weights until his late teens. To commence lifting weights at too early an age may lead to injuries, especially when overloading the epiphyses of the joints, and retard growth.

The schedule for hammer throwing will revolve around a few major exercises, these being 1) Power Clean, 2) Snatch, 3) Front Squat, 4) Back Squat, 5) High Pulls (clean and snatch grips), 6) Push Press. Some coaches favour the dead lift and 'Good Mornings' as major exercises (e.g. Bondarchuk).

Assistance exercises must be included in the hammer thrower's weight training programme. Considerable work must be done on the mid section of the body, since the force generated by the legs must be transferred to the shoulders and arms by the mid section.

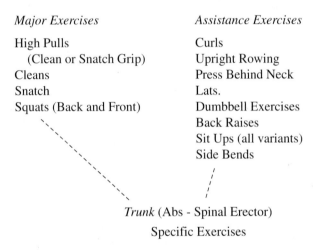

Major Exercises

High Pulls
  (Clean or Snatch Grip)
Cleans
Snatch
Squats (Back and Front)

Assistance Exercises

Curls
Upright Rowing
Press Behind Neck
Lats.
Dumbbell Exercises
Back Raises
Sit Ups (all variants)
Side Bends

Trunk (Abs - Spinal Erector)

Specific Exercises

Rest during Major Exercises – 2/3 minutes full recovery. Rest during Assistance Exercises – 1 minute between sets.

Example of Weight Training Programme

L denotes Light, M - Medium, H - Heavy.

<u>**WEEK 1**</u>   Major Exercises.

Monday	Snatch (L)	Clean Pull (M)	Back Squat (H)
	5 x 10 x ?	5 x 10 x ?	5 x 10 x ?
	e.g. for Back Squat	10 x 100kg increasing each set	
		10 x 110kg	
		10 x 120kg	
		10 x 130kg	
		10 x 140kg	

Assistance Exercises – Select 3/4 – 4 sets of 10 reps..

Wednesday	Front Squat (L)	Clean (M)	Snatch Pull (H)
	5 x 10	5 x 10	5 x 10

Assistance Exercises – Select 3/4 – 4 sets of 10 reps..

Friday	Back Squat (M)	Snatch (H)	Clean Pull (L)
	5 x 10	5 x 10	5 x 10

Assistance Exercises – Select 3/4 – 4 sets of 10 reps..

WEEK 2

Monday	Front Squat (M)	Clean (H)	Snatch Pull (L)
	6 x 10	6 x 10	6 x 10

Assistance Exercises – Select 3/4 – 5 sets of 10 reps..

Wednesday	Back Squat (L)	Snatch (M)	Clean Pull (H)
	6 x 10	6 x 10	6 x 10

Assistance Exercises – Select 3/4 – 5 sets of 10 reps..

Friday	Front Squat (H)	Clean (L)	Snatch Pull (M)
	6 x 10	6 x 10	6 x 10

Assistance Exercises – Select 3/4 – 5 sets of 10 reps..

Then repeat to complete a four week cycle; all poundages should have increased and then the repetitions changed as previously suggested (5 sets of 5 reps.). With the aforementioned schedule, it will be readily seen that each major exercise is only performed at 100% every two weeks. For a deeper insight into strength training, and for other schedules, an excellent publication is "Strength Training" by BAF National Coach, Max Jones.

Weight Throwing

Weight throwing from a standing position affords excellent development of special strength and power for the hammer thrower. Particular emphasis must be placed on the legs and hips during the throw – especially the hips where a good thrusting movement is essential.

Weights vary depending on the strength and maturity of the athlete. A mature athlete can use a 16kg weight during the preparation period and $12^1/_2$kg weight during the competition period. Younger athletes can safely use light weights and this is good for their development. Such weights can easily be made up by an engineer and can follow any dimensions (see Plate No. 17 – next page). For youngsters a hammer head with a handle attached is ideal.

EXERCISES

1. Weight Throw (Forwards) Plates No. 18a/18b overleaf.

2. Weight Throw (Vertical) Plates No. 19a/19b.

3. Weight Throw from the ground, across body and release over shoulder. Plates No. 20a/20b.

4. Weight Throw from shoulder level, down across front of body and release over the other shoulder. Grip weight in the right hand. Support on the hand of a bent left arm. Swing down and across the body and release over right shoulder. Plates No. 21a/21b.

Plate 17

Both sides of the body must be exercised – 4 or 6 throws to the right, then 4-6 throws to the left. In respect of vertical throwing the same applies, 4 or 6 throws with right hand followed by 4 or 6 throws with the left. Other exercises can also be performed, for example, backwards overhead.

Elastic Strength

Gains in gross strength are easily achieved; however, it is the amount of elastic strength plus technique that dictates the distance a hammer is thrown. Elastic strength is achieved via:

a) Lifting weights in an explosive manner.

b) Bounding/Jumping – e.g. standing long jump, standing triple jump, bounding, two legged hops (bunnies), hurdle jumping, depth jumping etc. A flat surface should be sought, preferably one with a little give.

c) Throwing heavy/light weights.

In the competitive season the volume of strength training will reduce to allow for quality work in other areas. It is important to ensure that strength levels are kept high during the season and that contact is kept with the weights. The athlete is only concerned with maintenance during this period. The athlete must ensure that he/she is fresh for competition and must not leave a training session drained of energy.

Planning Training

All the component parts that go to make up a hammer thrower's schedule must now be put together. The novice thrower requires a programme that does not vary a great deal, whereas the more advanced athlete will follow a programme which will reflect the time of the year.

Plate 18a

Plate 18b

Plate 19a

Plate 19b

Plate 20a

Plate 20b

Plate 21a

Plate 21b

Initially, the programme should be planned as a yearly cycle of training (macrocycle). It should be planned to culminate in a small number of competitions in which peak performance is desired. Peak performance should be aimed for at the most important competitions of the season.

It therefore follows that the yearly programme should be planned backwards from the time at which peak performance is desired. The training year should commence in October of the year preceding that in which the peak performance is desired. The training load should start at relatively easy levels and progress by stages to the optimum training loads. Full potential will only be realised after several years of systematic training, each session building a bigger base.

Before giving examples of schedules, it is important to stress to all athletes, whether a novice or international, that they must go through a warm-up routine to ensure that the body is prepared to perform and have less chance of incurring injury. The warm-up follows a sequence of activities which should become engrained early in the athlete's career.

The warm-up should start off with a jog in order that the body temperature be raised. The distance will vary, but 400m ought to be the minimum. Then follows two or three strides over 40 metres with a walk back recovery. Thereafter, general stretching exercises, followed by specific stretching exercises for hammer. In competitions, warm-up throws should be kept to a minimum and must be easy and relaxed.

Whilst not often witnessed amongst hammer throwers, a cool-down at the end of the training session or competition is also important. Its purpose is two-fold:

(1) Waste products accumulate as a result of intensive activity and this assists in their removal.

(2) It gives an opportunity to reflect on the training session or competition. The cool-down can be reversed from the warm-up with fewer exercises and repetitions being performed.

The Novice Thrower

First of all, let me deal with the novice thrower, 12-14 years of age. Within the initial preparation stage, certain basic principles of training must be adhered to. These are set out on page 21 (Teaching the Beginner in Chapter 7).

Training methods to be undertaken to achieve the basic principles include:

(1) Running & jumping exercises.

(2) Sprinting, games involving sprinting and relay racing.

(3) Throwing light implements – 4kg and less – off one, two, three and four turns.

(4) Throwing shots 4-5kg from various positions.

(5) Standing jumps.

(6) Multiple turning with a hammer on a flat strip.

The coach must be very mindful that the young athlete might well be doing several hours of strenuous physical activity at school. This is particularly so if he is a good games player. The amount of physical education performed by the athlete in school must be ascertained. Generally speaking, the average 12-14 year old will have sufficient endurance work during the school's P.E. programme.

The young athlete should not specialise too early, but be encouraged to try a variety of events – **FUN IS A MUST.**

Sample Schedule for the Novice Athlete

	WINTER (October - April)	**SUMMER** (May - August)
Sunday	i) Basic technique work – drills with sticks/rods etc.	i) Technique work – with pick-axe handle/rod etc. Turns and delivery from the statuesque position. (20 minutes)
	ii) Throwing – 15-20 throws with hammer. 15-20 throws with shot (various positions).	ii) 15 throws working for rhythm and relaxation.
	iii) Jumping – up to 30 multi jumps.	iii) 12 shot throws for delivery – 6 either side into net, or from various other positions.
	iv) Second event work, e.g. sprinting or 5 runs over 4 flights of hurdles.	iv) Obstacle race involving jumping and sprinting plus balance (plank walk).
Monday	REST	REST
Tuesday	i) 20 minutes stretching with club group.	i) Throwing – 20 throws working for smooth rotation, rhythm and relaxation.
	ii) Circuit training – general nature.	ii) Sprinting – 60m x 4
Wednesday	REST	REST
Thursday	i) Basic technique work – drills with pick-axe handle, rods etc.	i) Technique with stick/rods 20 mins.
	ii) 12-15 hammer throws	ii) Throwing – 15-20 off 2/3/4 turns.

Thursday (cont'd)	iii) Circuit training.	iii) Long jumping (6 stride approach x 8).
Friday	REST	REST
Saturday	School Match	Club or School Competition

	or	or
	i) 12-15 hammer throws	i) Throwing – 15-20 off 2/3/4 turns
	ii) Shot throwing – various positions.	ii) Shot throwing – various positions.
	iii) Other athletic activity, e.g. sprinting/hurdling/jumping.	ii) Sprinting.

Intermediate Thrower – 15/18 years of age

Having trained two years or more in the novice stage, throwers ought to be able to throw proficiently from 3 or 4 turns. In addition, they should have a good basic knowledge of the technique, and be able to display the requirements of the double support and single support phases of the throw within their technique. The basis of an effective delivery ought also be evident.

The following tasks should be tackled in the intermediate stage:

1) Improving hammer throwing technique.
2) Developing special physical qualities (speed and strength).
3) Developing psychological and tactical abilities.

The training methods to be undertaken to achieve the aforementioned tasks, will include:

a) Throwing light, normal and heavy hammers from 3 or 4 turns.
b) Throwing implements of varying weights (from 6kg to $12^1/_2$ kg) by various means from the standing position.
c) A minimum of strength training with weights and special exercises.
d) Jumps.
e) Sprints.

Sample Schedule for 13 Year Old of Several Years Experience

Period	Strength	Specific Strength	Elastic Strength	Endurance	Technique	Rest
Oct/Nov (6 weeks)	General exercises 3-4 sets of 8-12 reps. (x 3/wk). N.B. Not heavy poundage.	Medicine ball work – high reps. – working on rotational strength (x 1/wk).	—	4000m steady run or conditioning bodyweight circuits (x3/wk). Bodyweight circuits after run.	—	1 day
Nov/Dec	Basic lifts 4 sets of 6 rising to 8 then adding weight (x 3/wk).	Medicine ball work as above (x 1/wk). Weight throwing from standing positions 9-12½kg x 32 reps. (8 of each exercise) (x 2/wk).	Bounding – 8 sets 3/5 bunnies 60m fast strides x 5 (x 2/wk).	3000m steady run (x 1 wk) Bodyweight circuit.	Throwing (x 2/wk) working on priority points.	1 day
Jan/March	Basic lifts 4 sets of 4 reps., rising to 6, then adding weight (x 3/wk).	Medicine ball work – as above (x 1/wk). Weight throwing from standing positions as above (x 2/wk).	Bounding 3 bunnies x 6 sets. 8 standing long jumps, 40m sprint x 5 reps. (x 1/wk).	2000m run at a good pace.	Throwing (x 3/wk) working on priority points.	1 day
April/May	As for Jan/March (x 3 wk).	As Jan/March.	Bounding 3 bunnies x 6 sets. 8 standing long jumps. 40m x 5 reps. (x 2/wk).	—	Throwing (x 3-4/wk).	1 day
June/August	Moderate poundage – weights handled explosively (x 1/2 wk).	—	Weight throwing – using a lighter weight handled explosively 4 sets of 8 reps. (x 1/wk). Bounding as for April/May (x 2/wk). Sprints (x 1/wk).		Throwing (x 4). Throwing (x 4).	1 day 1 day

NOTE: FOR THE REASONS ALREADY SET OUT, THE YOUNG ATHLETE MUST NOT LIFT HEAVY WEIGHTS.

Sample Schedule for Advanced Thrower – Single Periodised Year (Athlete in Full Employment)

Period	Strength	Specific Strength	Elastic Strength	Endurance	Technique	Rest
Oct/Nov.	Follow programme as set out in Strength Training (Pages 34-36) for all periods until June (x 3/wk).	Medicine ball work – high reps. working on rotational strength (x 1/wk).	—	4000m run (x 2/wk) Bodyweight circuit (x 2/wk).	—	1 day
Nov/Dec.	Ongoing as per schedule.	Medicine ball work – as above (x 1 wk). Weight throwing from standing positions 16kg x 48 reps. (12 of each exercise) (x 2/wk).	Power bounding (x 2 wk).	6 x 100m (x 2 wk).	Major skill changes with light hammer $6^{1}/_4$ or $6^{3}/_4$ kg. Heavy hammer 9kg-10kg (x 2/wk).	1day
Jan/March	Ongoing as per schedule.	Medicine ball as above (x 1/wk). Weight throwing as above (x 2/wk).	Bounding 6-8 fast contacts (x 2/wk). 40m sprints x 6 reps. (x 2/wk).	—	Throwing with $6^{1}/_4$ kg or $6^{3}/_4$ kg hammer for technique improvement. Remainder of throwing for period $7^{1}/_4$ kg (35%) 8kg(35%) 9kg (30%) (x 3/wk) $12^{1}/_2$kg or 16kg 1 metre in length an additional option.	1 day

Table continues on next page

Sample Schedule for Advanced Thrower – Single Periodised Year (Athlete in Full Employment) (cont'd)

Period	Strength	Specific Strength	Elastic Strength	Endurance	Technique	Rest
April/May	Ongoing as per schedule.	Weight throwing 16kg x 48reps.. (x 2/wk).	Bounding – 6 fast contacts phasing down to 3 fast contacts (x 1/wk) 30-40m sprints x 6 reps. (x 1/wk).	—	Throwing 6¼ kg (10%) 7¼ kg (60%) 8kg (17½%) 9kg (12½%) (x 3-4/wk) Additional optional 12½ kg (1 metre) or 16kg (1 metre).	1 day
June/August	Maintenance Explosive work 5 x 5 reps. (page 34) 6 sets (x 3/wk).	Weight throwing 12½kg x 36 reps.. Explosive.	Bounding low volume/ high quality 1-2-3 fast contacts (x 2wk) 4 x 30m sprints (x 1/wk).	—	Mainly 7¼ kg (x 4-5/wk) Working rhythm and form. Also 6¼ or 6¾ kg or heavy hammer on short wire.	1 day

Chapter 9

THE ORGANISATION OF TEACHING AND TRAINING

Although the skill progressions of teaching and coaching hammer have already been well covered in the preceding chapters, it is important that some space is devoted to the safe organisation of teaching and coaching groups.

In essence the hammer is no more dangerous than either discus or javelin. Throwing from within a proper safety cage obviously provides the safest possible conditions, but it must be remembered that it does not guarantee absolute safety. When working with reasonably large groups of throwers the presence of a cage can often be a hindrance, since it slows the frequency of throws and thereby involvement and motivation on the part of the throwers. In this way the learning climate is diminished.

Provided that the group stand opposite the hammer's low point, well back from the thrower, and watch the throw as it is being made, training can take place without the use of a cage with the same safety guarantees as in discus and javelin undertaken under similar conditions.

A safety precaution commonly used in discus coaching is to arrange the group in echelon (Diagram 2). This removes the person on each thrower's right well back from the possible line of flight if the throw is 'sliced'. Left-handed throwers are placed at the left-hand side of the group. Identical arrangements are an added aid to safety when teaching groups of hammer throwers without a cage.

Careful maintenance of hammers (see Chapter 4) and cages prevents those accidents which may result from breakage. In almost 70% of such incidents, which do happen, poor maintenance of equipment, allied to poor siting of facilities, is a major contributory factor. The BAF and the National Playing Fields Association publish further advisory information on hammer safety.

The major aims in teaching a group of novice throwers should be:

1. To make the teaching so enjoyable and challenging that the class comes back for more.
2. To teach only those essentials of technique that are necessary to achieve this.
3. To provide opportunities for lots of practice *in safe conditions.*

These aims cannot be achieved by making thirty potential throwers queue for the use of a single circle. It was partly in order to avoid this mistake that the 'short hammer' teaching method (described in Chapter 7) was devised. By removing the wire, control over the hammer is increased, and the range which it travels is reduced to similar proportions to those obtaining in shot putt. This makes it possible for many more people to throw in a given area, so making it most suitable for mass instruction.

The ultimate in practice facilities should ensure that a number of throwers are so distributed over the training area that they are in effect alone. In this way the possibility of each thrower injuring someone else, or being injured by someone else, is eliminated. This is not as difficult to achieve as it may at first appear. Four throwers can be safely dispersed around a space such as a soccer or rugby pitch as in Diagram 3, provided that none is throwing more than 40 metres. An alternative provision for four throwers, utilising a simple cage, is shown in Diagram 4. Such arrangements, with metal mesh cages no more than seven feet high, are quite common in European countries.

Echelon formation for safer group teaching of hammer

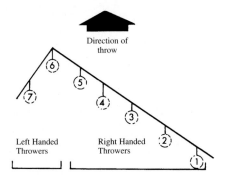

Diagram 2

Dispersal of throwing area around a games pitch
(N.B. All sectors should have an angle of 40°)

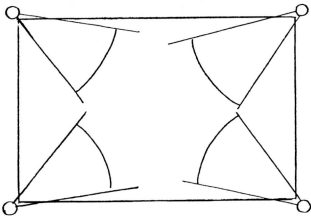

Diagram 3

Safe arrangement of four throwing circles separated by a simple cage

(N.B. All sectors should have an angle of 40°)

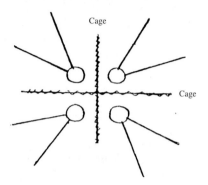

Diagram 4

When groups are working together it is vital that they wait until all have thrown before retrieving. It is even safer if this is carried out under the direction of an appointed leader, or of the teacher/coach. In addition each thrower *must* assume the extra responsibility of ensuring that the landing area is absolutely clear before he throws.

Where possible it is useful practice to mark and maintain distance arcs at 10 metre intervals beyond 30 or 40 metres so that ready assessment of performance is possible, and so that the throwers are motivated by their successes.

Chapter 10

BITS AND PIECES

There is much evidence to support the view that a greater percentage of longest throws are made during rounds 1 and 2 of a hammer competition than in any other rounds. The notion of 'coming from behind' is statistically not well supported. It is therefore prudent to prepare for competition with this very much in mind.

During the final week leading up to the competition strenuous training, such as very heavy weight lifting, or long throwing sessions, should be removed as far away from the day of competition as possible, i.e. to the Monday or Tuesday preceding. As the competition draws nearer so the volume of work should be reduced. Throwing hammers lighter than the competition implement can help to improve the 'feel' for the hammer when the competition finally takes place.

Some athletes take two full days rest immediately before the competition day, while others only take one – a small number don't take any. It is important to emphasise the speed and wholeness of the throw during these final training sessions so that the dynamic elements of the competitive throw are rehearsed.

The day immediately before the competition should be used for getting organised. Kit should be packed and include such additional items as hammer shoes, hammer glove, Venice turpentine for treating the glove to make it sticky or magnesium carbonate to dry it off, PVC insulation tape for taping finger ends under the glove, spare shoe laces and safety pins. If possible it is useful to have two pairs of throwing shoes – one pair with a smooth sole for slow circles, and one pair with rough soles for very fast circles. Tracksuits, vests, shorts, socks and wet suits are normal athletic equipment and should be automatically packed for a meeting. Finally, don't forget the meeting programme and admission card.

If the thrower possesses a hammer of his own it should be taken with him. It should be checked to see that it is in good order, i.e. that the spindle is free running, that the wire is absolutely straight, and that it is the correct weight and *maximum* overall length. Small adjustments to achieve this are possible by either adding a little more weight under the spindle (a grub screw is used to hold the spindle in place, and once this is removed it is possible to unscrew the whole assembly) or by taping a small nail to the wire. Adjustments to hammer length can be made either by fitting a slightly longer wire or by stretching the handle with the aid of a vice.

On the day of competition travel should be arranged so that there is time to spare, just in case of breakdown or unexpected delay, and so that the athlete arrives at the track well in advance of the starting time. Time will be needed for changing, collecting numbers, warm-up and reporting.

The amount of actual throwing that is done in warm-up will be very individual, and related to past experience. The athlete should do as much as suits him. However, bearing in mind all that has been written about the importance of the first throws, it is advisable to plan warm-up so that it enables him to achieve this. Current thinking leans most heavily towards total abstinence from throwing during warm-up in order to avoid draining up the benefits that can be derived from anticipation of the competition.

Diet

The dietary requirements of the hammer thrower are very important, especially in this day and age when training levels are becoming more and more demanding, and when modern methods of food production are actually reducing its nutritional value. The levels of intake will need to relate to the thrower's employment, and to the amount of training that he undertakes, and its energy expenditure.

The energy value of food is measured in calories, as is the requirement of the athlete. Someone doing office work will have an energy requirement equal to 2500 cals, on average, whereas a heavy manual worker will require as many as 3500 cals. Add to that the requirements of a training programme occupying six days per week, and including three sessions of lifting at 85% maximum totalling 60 to 100 tonnes per month, and the total energy needs may reach 5000-6000 cals per day, particularly if it is also necessary to gain weight.

Within these parameters a reasonably varied diet will ensure that the balance between carbohydrates, proteins and fats is correct. The right ratio is 5:4:1. Those athletes who are tempted to follow fashion and consume large amounts of protein in order to put on weight would do well to remember that if they do not meet their energy requirements from a carbohydrate source, then the protein is used to make good the deficit. This is tantamount to putting five star petrol into a car that requires two star petrol – it is money up the exhaust pipe. The normal protein requirement is equivalent to 1 gm of protein per day per kg of bodyweight.

Coaching

Other than competing, the greatest personal satisfaction that the sport can offer comes through successful coaching. Coaching differs from teaching in that it involves personal supervision and contact with a single athlete rather than the mass approach. Detailed attention to an individual's needs in skill acquistion, conditioning, and competition then assumes prime importance. Good coaching at a high level of performance is time consuming and requires the following qualities of the coach:

1. A sound knowledge of the event.
2. Photographic powers of observation, coupled with the capacity to make critical analysis of what he sees.
3. Ability to communicate with the athlete – part of which involves an ability to verbalise sensations.
4. Consistency and reliability.
5. An enquiring mind and burning desire to improve his own knowledge and thereby his athlete.
6. Eternal optimism whilst remaining a realist.

BIBLIOGRAPHY

1. Hammer Throwing – Carl Johnson (BAF).

2. Hints for Beginner Hammer Throwers – A. Bondarchuk. (The Throws, 4th edition – Jess Carver.)

3. The Main Elements of Modern Hammer Throwing Technique – Eberhard Gaeda. (The Throws, 4th edition – Jess Carver.)

4. The Hammer Throw – Eberhard Gaeda. (New Studies in Athletics – Vol. 5. Iss. No.1. , March 1990 – IAAF.)

5. Theoretical Aspects of Training Control for Highly Qualified Throwers – J. Bakarinov. (New Studies in Athletics – Vol. 5. Iss. No.1. March 1990 – IAAF.)

6. Hammer Throw – Biomechanical Analysis of Yuri Sedykh – Ralph M. Ottos. (New Studies in Athletics – Vol. 7, Iss. No.2. September 1992 – IAAF.)

7. Biomechanical Analysis of the Hammer Throw 1994. (AAA/WAAA Championships plus European Cup) – Calvin Morriss and Roger Bartlett.

8. Strength Training – Max Jones (BAF).

9. Mobility Training – Norman Brook (BAF).

10. 'The Thrower' magazine – Max Jones.

	Hammer Throw		Pha
–	A	B	Final s prior to
C	D	E	Transit first tur
F	G	H	Double phase

			Reference	Points to be observed
B		1.	Head	Held high.
B		2.	Trunk	Upright – maximum torque.
B		3.	Legs	Slightly bent.
D	E	4.	Head	Looking in direction of hammer.
		5.	Arms	Left arm extended. Right arm bent.
D	E	6.	Arms	Extended to form a shoulder arm triangle
D		7.	Hammer	Almost at entry point.
D	E	8.	Trunk	Slight forward inclination.
D	E	9.	Knees	Bent and in sitting position.
D	E	10.	Pivot leg	Inward rotation on heel.
D	E	11.	Trail leg	Delayed on ball of foot.
D	E	12.	Body weight	Over both legs.
G	H	13.	Head	Direction hammer.
G	H	14.	Arms	Working hammer through frontal plane.
		15.	Hammer	High over head on right.
G		16.	Hammer	Prior to low point.
	H	17.	Hammer	After low point.
		18.	Trunk	Max. torque (shoulder/pelvis).
G	H	19.	Trunk	Slight backward inclination.
G	H	20.	Hips	Pressing actively in turning direction.
		21.	Knees	Bent right knee slightly; left knee considerably. (Centre of gravity lowered as a result.)

continued on pages 54 & 55

Hammer Throw   *Ph*

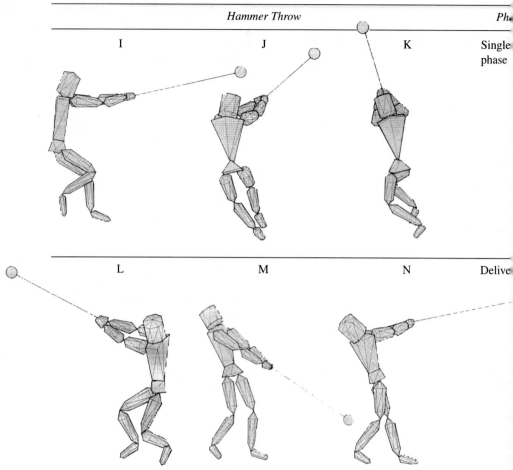

I	J	K	Single phase
L	M	N	Delive

		Reference		Points to be observed
J	K	22.	Head	Direction hammer.
J	K	23.	Arms	Extended. Passive.
		24.	Hammer	Pushed far to the left.
J	K	25.	Hammer	Prior to and at high point.
J	K	26.	Trunk	Slight backward inclination.
		27.	Pivot leg	Active turning on heel.
		28.	Trail leg	Lifted.
J	K	29.	Pivot leg	Bent at knee – on ball
J	K	30.	Trail leg	Bent and actively turning.

		31.	Head	Direction hammer.
M	N	32.	Head	Thrown back.
M	N	33.	Arms	Work hammer through frontal plane.
		34.	Trunk	Upright.
M	N	35.	Trunk	Slight backward inclination.
	N	36.	Hips	Extended.
		37.	Knees	Bent.
	N	38.	Pivot leg	Extended on heel (foot platformed).
	N	39.	Trail leg	On toe – slightly bent.
	N	40.	Left side	Blocked.

Swings and Entry

Entry plus Turns 1 and 2

Turn 3 and Delivery